to: _____

from: _____

Published by Sellers Publishing, Inc.

161 John Roberts Road, South Portland, ME 04106
Visit us at www.sellerspublishing.com • E-mail: rsp@rsvp.com

Copyright © 2014 Sellers Publishing, Inc.
All rights reserved.

Editor: Robin Haywood
Photo Editors: Mary Baldwin, Amanda Mooney
Design: Mary Baldwin, Patti Urban

ISBN 13: 978-1-4162-4521-6

Printed and bound in China.

Cover image © 2014 Deanna Cathcart

10 9 8 7 6 5 4 3 2 1

pooped puppies

life's too short to work like a dog

SELLERS
PUBLISHING

Anything that can't be
done in bed isn't worth
doing at all.

Groucho Marx

Work is not always required.
There is such a thing as
sacred idleness.

George MacDonald

I slip from workaholic to bum real easy.

Matthew Broderick

Naps are nature's
way of reminding
you that life is nice
— like a beautiful,
softly swinging
hammock strung
between birth
and infinity.

Peggy Noonan

Sundays; quiet islands on
the tossing seas of life.

S. W. Duffield

I don't generally feel anything until noon; then it's time for my nap.

Bob Hope

I have long been of the opinion that if work were such a splendid thing the rich would have kept more of it for themselves.

Bruce Grocott

17

Tension is who you think you should be. Relaxation is who you are.

Chinese proverb

Think what a better world it would be if we all, the whole world, had milk and cookies about three o'clock every afternoon and then lay down on our blankets for a nap.

Barbara Jordan

Sleeping is no mean art: for its sake
one must stay awake all day.

Friedrich Nietzsche

Work is the refuge
of those who have
nothing better to do.

Oscar Wilde

25

Nothing cures
insomnia like the
realization that it's
time to get up.

Author unknown

Learning to ignore
things is one of
the great paths
to inner peace.

Robert J. Sawyer

Sometimes the most
important moment
in a whole day is the
rest we take between
two deep breaths.

Etty Hillesum

To sit with a dog on a hillside on a glorious afternoon is to be back in Eden, where doing nothing was not boring — it was peace.

Milan Kundera

Consciousness:
that annoying time
between naps.

Author unknown

I don't have anything against work. I just figure, why deprive somebody who really loves it.

Dobie Gillis

I love sleep. My life has the tendency to fall apart when I'm awake, you know?

Ernest Hemingway

If you are losing your leisure,
look out, you may be losing
your soul.

Anonymous

No day is so bad it can't
be fixed with a nap.

Carrie Snow

Sometimes opportunity knocks, but most of the time it sneaks up and then quietly steals away.

Doug Larson

I try to take it one day
at a time, but sometimes
several days attack me
all at once.

Jennifer Yane

The mark of a successful person is one who has spent an entire day on the bank of a river without feeling guilty about it.

Author unknown

How beautiful it is to do nothing, and then to rest afterward.

Spanish proverb

If people
concentrated
on the really
important things
in life, there'd be
a shortage of
fishing poles.

Doug Larson

If your dreams turn
to dust . . . vacuum.

Author unknown

Sitting quietly,
doing nothing,
spring comes and
the grass grows
by itself.

Zen proverb

Sometimes it's important
to work for that pot of
gold. But other times it's
essential to take time off
and to make sure that your
most important decision in
the day simply consists of
choosing which color of
the rainbow to slide down.

Douglas Pagels

Life is something that happens when you can't get to sleep.

Fran Lebowitz

I like work; it fascinates me. I can sit and look at it for hours.

Jerome K. Jerome

Credits

Cover image: © 2014 Deanna Cathcart

pp. 4-5 photo © 2014 Neo Vision/Getty; pp. 6-7 photo © 2014 Aflo; pp. 8-9 photo © 2014 Larry Allen/Bruce Coleman, Inc.; pp. 10-11 photo © 2014 Deanna Cathcart; pp.12-13 photo © 2014 Deanna Cathcart; pp. 14-15 photo © 2014 Bob Elsdale/Workbook; pp. 16-17 © 2014 David Muscroft/SuperStock; pp. 18-19 photo © 2014 Takashi Yamazaki/A.collection/amana; pp. 20-21 photo © 2014 Aflo; pp. 22-23 photo © 2014 Jim Craigmyle/Corbis; pp. 24-25 photo © 2014 Akira Matoba/SuperStock; pp. 26-27 photo © 2014 Akira.M/maria/A.collection/amana; pp. 28-29 photo © 2014 Aflo; pp. 30-31 photo © 2014 Neo Vision/Getty; pp 32-33 photo © 2014 Akira.M/maria/A.collection/amana; pp. 34-35 photo © 2014 Jacob Mosser/Positive Images; pp. 36-37 photo © 2014 Corbis; pp. 38-39 photo © 2014 Deanna Cathcart; pp. 40-41 photo © 2014 Deanna Cathcart; pp. 42-43 photo © 2014 Aflo; pp. 44-45 photo © 2014 Corbis; pp. 46-47 photo © 2014 Jay Syverson/Corbis; pp. 48-49 photo © 2014 Akira.M/maria/A.collection/amana; pp. 50-51 photo © 2014 Elizabeth Flynn/S&E Photo; pp. 52-53 photo © 2014 Aflo; pp. 54-55 photo © 2014 L.W.A./Workbook; pp. 56-57 photo © 2014 Aflo; pp. 58-59 © 2014 Jim Zuckerman/Corbis; pp. 60-61 photo © Alley Cat Productions/PictureQuest; pp. 62-63 photo © 2014 E.A. Janes/Age Fotostock.